1,000,000 Books

are available to read at

Forgotten Books

www.ForgottenBooks.com

Read online
Download PDF
Purchase in print

ISBN 978-0-260-29264-3
PIBN 11176696

This book is a reproduction of an important historical work. Forgotten Books uses state-of-the-art technology to digitally reconstruct the work, preserving the original format whilst repairing imperfections present in the aged copy. In rare cases, an imperfection in the original, such as a blemish or missing page, may be replicated in our edition. We do, however, repair the vast majority of imperfections successfully; any imperfections that remain are intentionally left to preserve the state of such historical works.

Forgotten Books is a registered trademark of FB &c Ltd.
Copyright © 2018 FB &c Ltd.
FB &c Ltd, Dalton House, 60 Windsor Avenue, London, SW19 2RR.
Company number 08720141. Registered in England and Wales.

For support please visit www.forgottenbooks.com

1 MONTH OF FREE READING

at

www.ForgottenBooks.com

By purchasing this book you are eligible for one month membership to ForgottenBooks.com, giving you unlimited access to our entire collection of over 1,000,000 titles via our web site and mobile apps.

To claim your free month visit: www.forgottenbooks.com/free1176696

* Offer is valid for 45 days from date of purchase. Terms and conditions apply.

English
Français
Deutsche
Italiano
Español
Português

www.forgottenbooks.com

Mythology Photography **Fiction**
Fishing Christianity **Art** Cooking
Essays Buddhism Freemasonry
Medicine **Biology** Music **Ancient Egypt** Evolution Carpentry Physics
Dance Geology **Mathematics** Fitness
Shakespeare **Folklore** Yoga Marketing
Confidence Immortality Biographies
Poetry **Psychology** Witchcraft
Electronics Chemistry History **Law**
Accounting **Philosophy** Anthropology
Alchemy Drama Quantum Mechanics
Atheism Sexual Health **Ancient History**
Entrepreneurship Languages Sport
Paleontology Needlework Islam
Metaphysics Investment Archaeology
Parenting Statistics Criminology
Motivational

ELLEN HANLY

OR

The True History

OF

THE COLLEEN BAWN

BY ONE WHO KNEW HER IN LIFE, AND SAW HER
IN DEATH

DUBLIN
MOFFAT & CO., 6 D'OLIER STREET
LONDON: HAMILTON, ADAMS & CO.
1868.

DUBLIN STEAM PRINTING COMPANY.

INTRODUCTION.

THE Author of this little volume, which is now presented to the public, is one of the very few survivors of those who took an active part in discovering the perpetrators of the revolting tragedy which gave rise to the interesting story of "The Collegians," by the late Gerald Griffin, and also afforded a ground-work for the drama of "The Colleen Bawn," which the lovers of theatricals in the United Kingdom have, for some time past, been viewing with rapturous delight. It may be thought very unromantic of the Author, who now, be it observed, takes upon him to give a history of *facts*, to dissipate the almost angelic halo which, no doubt, in many a young mind, invests the seraphic character of "The Colleen Bawn," but, humble as was her origin, and sad as was her death, the melting scenes which, perhaps, drew tears from many a lovely eye, and raised tender emotions in many a throbbing heart, in witnessing the drama wrought out from this interesting story, would vanish into utter nothingness when contrasted with the tremendous reality, witnessed nearly half a century ago by the Author, from whose memory, the young blooming face of the original, in the midst of life and health (whose voice is still sounding in his ears), and the horrible mutilated corpse, of that once lovely young creature, can never be obliterated.

For some time past it has been my purpose to give to the public my recollection of the facts connected with this real tragedy, but long-continued illness, and a series of domestic afflictions, have prevented me, until now, from completing what I had some time since commenced. With all the defects of a writer of little pretension, and very inadequately trained in the mysteries of authorship, I now commit my little volume to a generous public. I cannot, of course, flatter myself that I shall escape criticism, perhaps severe in its strictures, but, whatever may be the result of appearing in print, I can truly testify that my object in writing this little history is a good one, and should any of those who peruse its pages feel interested in the facts, which, as well as memory, after the lapse of nearly half a century can recall them, are faithfully recorded, I only pray that what I write may tend to their edification, and be the means of preserving them from every evil way.

THE COLLEEN BAWN.

CHAPTER I.

EARLY in the summer of 1819, I doffed my cap and gown in my rooms at dear old Trinity, and, with elastic step and buoyant spirits, issued from the ancient gate-way of "*Alma Mater*," filled with bright visions of the fun and frolic, the rural sports, and manly exercises of the country, anticipating, with feelings of no ordinary delight, the sweet society of the loved relatives of home, which I hoped to enjoy during the long vacation, now commenced. Having bidden a kind farewell to the college porters, whom I always made my friends, and who, as I departed, respectfully raised their caps from their brows, and with a hearty cheer wished me a merry time in the country and a safe return, I bounded off, accompanied by my skip,* with my trunk on his back, and reached the office of the two-day coach for Limerick, just as my old friend Jim Dempsey (alongside whom I drove many a journey in the summer's heat and in the winter's cold) had taken his seat on the box. I always made it a point, and trust I shall continue to do so, to act with courtesy, and to exercise the law of kindness towards all with whom it has been, or may be, my lot to hold intercourse while passing through the varying scenes of this eventful world; and I strongly recommend every one who wishes to enjoy real happiness, to cultivate the same spirit. By acting so I have made many a rough way smooth, I have softened the naturally sullen and uncourteous dispositions of several, who, if treated with hauteur, would probably have resented it, and I secured for myself the friendship of many who, through a kind

* The student's servants were called "skips" in my college days.

word spoken in due season, were led to see the folly and misery of giving way to unruly tempers. The moment my old friend Jim got a glimpse of me, he gave me a knowing wink, and made some palavering excuse to a stout rustic (whom, in his rich Irish dialect, he called a Feeltough*) that had pre-occupied the box seat, and, having prevailed on him to give way, quickly arranged a comfortable place at his side for the young collegian who had often fought gallantly with him against the winter's storm and the cutting breeze. No sooner had I taken the place which my friend Jim had so adroitly provided for me, than " crack went the whip, round went the wheels," and away we bowled at the rate of six Irish miles an hour, a slapping pace fifty years ago, when railroads were not so much as thought of. After a comfortable journey of about nine hours, not marked by any particular incident, but very much enlivened by the racy and amusing jests of my jolly and good-humoured companion Jim, we

* A wild mountaineer.

arrived at Mountrath in time to partake of a most substantial and well served dinner; and, after it, to enjoy for the evening the society of the passengers of the up, as well as those of the down coach, which for many years had daily met at that provincial town. Short as the time was at these social meetings for communion amongst the passengers, friendships were formed, and, no doubt, tender engagements commenced which ended only with life. Looking back to those happy days, when the youthful heart was seldom crushed with care, and the merry students of our noble and ancient University, after shaking off the dust of nine months' collegiate life, were hastening homewards to brace their nerves for the winter term, I confess that I recur to them with the most pleasurable feelings. Though, no doubt, there were in those days of often exuberant wildness, many things done which it would have been better to have left undone, still, in my opinion, there is nothing better qualified to prepare young men for the battle of life than the rough usage which they will often meet at school and at college. Having been roused from our slumbers at five the next morning by the shrill voice of the well-known *Snowball* (who had received that soubriquet, the direct contrast to his Ethiopian skin,) sounding in our ears the words, which many a weary traveller would heartily have wished had been postponed, " Time to rise, Massa," we had the alternative to shake off Mr. Murphy* and pack up for another long day's drive to Limerick, or to be left behind. We started precisely at six, and arrived at Dunkerran at nine, well prepared for a hearty breakfast, for which we paid two tenpennies, with a trifle to the waiter, and, depend upon it, left little profit to the " Maitre d' hotel." The incidents of the journey I shall at present sum up, by merely stating, that, having left my friend Jim at Mountrath, his successor, though equally civil and accommodating, was sombre and reserved in his nature, a strong contrast to my jolly friend

* The Irishism for Morpheus, the god of sleep.

whom we had left behind. Having arrived safely at Limerick at three P.M., I walked about the town with a beloved college friend and companion, alas, now no more! and exchanged kind and affectionate salutations with numerous acquaintances, and thus whiled away the time till six o'clock, when I enjoyed, with my friend just alluded to, a hearty dinner at Moriarty's, now Cruises', Hotel: looking forward with earnest longings for the morrow, at the close of which, after a sail down the Shannon, I hoped to clasp to my bosom the beloved friends for whom my youthful heart for the last nine months was deeply and intensely longing.

An incident occurred that night in Limerick which memory still retains with feelings of thankfulness to Almighty God, for making me an humble instrument in His hands for saving from perhaps a horrible death a whole family, who were then slumbering, unconscious of their danger, and totally unaware that their house was on fire. I was walking, with my friend before alluded to, through

Cecil Street, about ten o'clock, when I saw a more than usual blaze of light in a house, and immediately accosting him said, "I am sure that house is on fire." I thought it better, therefore, even though I should be mistaken, to rouse the inmates; and, to do so, I thundered with all my might at the door, and, after a lapse of a minute or two, it was opened by a terrified and half-dressed maidservant. We did not wait to exchange words with the domestic, but rushed up stairs, and having forced in the drawing-room door, flames immediately burst out, and finding the carpet and several other articles in a blaze, we set heartily to work, shouting the while for help, and, with God's assistance, were soon enabled to check the progress of the devouring element, and eventually completely to extinguish it. We were in the midst of our work of mercy, when two half-dressed females, evidently of the higher class, made their appearance on the stairs, and, though we used every exertion to soothe their fears by assuring them that all danger was at an end, the terror which they had experienced was so intense that they both swooned away, and it was some time before they recovered from the shock which they had received. I know not whether any of the parties, besides myself, who went through this fiery trial are now alive, but, should they be, and this brief account of the occurrence, which was so near being fatal to them, meet their eye, they will, no doubt, remember the young striplings, fresh from college, who were providentially made the instruments of saving their lives.

CHAPTER II.

I shall now enter into the details of the fearful tragedy which I have undertaken to relate, and which, at the time it was enacted, occupied a very prominent place amongst the extraordinary events of the day; especially from the position in life of the principal malefactor. This ruthless villain was clearly convicted of one of the most heartless murders on record in the annals of civilized life, and for which, in the very county where he ought to have maintained a highly respectable station, he deservedly suffered the extreme penalty of the law. Ellen Hanly, the unfortunate victim of this brutal murder, was the daughter of a small farmer, and, at the time she eloped with this fiend in human shape, was residing with an uncle, a respectable tradesman, who, by honest industry and economy, had accumulated a sum of about sixty pounds. Her heartless seducer persuaded poor Elly to steal this money from her kind protector, who, it will appear from the sequel, was most devotedly attached to this lovely young creature, whom he had adopted as his child, and brought up from her infancy with the most tender care. I had partly from her own lips the history of her misfortune, which originated in listening to the persuasive eloquence of her well-trained seducer, who had promised her marriage before she fled with him from the house of her affectionate uncle, and which pledge she felt quite convinced he had redeemed to the fullest extent by making her his wife.

Shortly after she had entrusted herself to the care of this vile wretch, he got up a mock marriage, which the poor young creature, in all her simplicity, imagined was perfectly genuine. This *gallant* son of Mars (for it appears he had been an officer in the Royal Marines) hired a villain, who was as accomplished in iniquity as himself, to personate a

Roman Catholic priest, and who, being robed in the vestments of a clergyman of that communion, performed the marriage ceremony; and thus not only satisfied the conscience of the unsuspecting young creature (who by her father's sworn testimony was under sixteen years of age), but also divested her of all suspicion of the nefarious plans of the *highbred* villain, who, when he had spent all the money which he had tempted his poor victim to abstract from her uncle, persuaded the accomplice of his deeds of darkness to murder, and to commit her body to the deep.

On the morning after my arrival in Limerick, with the scene of the previous night vividly before me, and romantic visions of the inmates of the house, whom I had been so fortunate as to rescue, floating in my boyish mind, I left the hotel to take my passage to G―― in the "Lady Frances" packet, the best mode of conveyance at that period, and to be preferred to bad roads and worse carriages. As soon as I came on board I was warmly greeted by Tom Mahoney, the pilot, who, during my schoolboy days at Kilrush, where his voyage ended, often bore a message from me to dear friends at home; and into whose sympathizing ears I often poured a flood of all the wrongs I *fancied* I had suffered, when the birch of our preceptor was exercised, as I firmly believed, with undue severity upon me for my *trifling* peccadillos. "Musha, Master D——," said old Tom, "I am glad to see your darling face once more. Wisha, faix you're grown a fine slashing fellow since last I saw you. In troth Paddy A—— would have something to do to hise* you now; I'd be bound you'd have a tug wid the ould lad before you'd let him put you up. Yerra! how is Master G—— and Master J——? Monnum! but they say Master J—— is the brightest boy in college; faix, the next pramium he gets, we'll have a *bonefire* for him in Kilrush." With these hearty, and, no doubt, sincere expressions of friendship for myself and kind

* To put a boy who was to be flogged on the back of another.

inquiries about my two beloved brothers, alas, now no more! (one of whom was a distinguished ornament of our noble University), my old and warm-hearted friend Tom, upon the skipper's giving orders to cast off the hawsers, took a stout hold of the tiller and got the little vessel under weigh. Just as she was gliding along the wharf, a tall, dark-visaged young man, evidently the worse of liquor, jumped on board with a gun in his hand, crying out, "Ha! I was near being late. Elly, dear," addressing a pretty young creature sitting on a bench on the deck, "What would you do if I were left behind? Hie ho! faith I was raking all night," he exclaimed, throwing his hands over his head, with the gun still firmly in his grasp, which he swung from one side to the other, to the evident dismay of the passengers, any of whom might, during one of his wild gyrations over the deck, have received the contents through his body. It was really a very ticklish position to be placed in, as the gun was loaded, of which I subsequently made myself sure by a trial, for, after he had made a few wild whirls round the vessel, he laid down the fowling-piece on the deck, threw himself exhausted on a stretcher, and when I found that he was buried in sleep I took it up and found it heavily charged.

We had now moved away from the quay, and with the ebbing tide were carried swiftly beyond the precincts of the fast retiring city; old Tom steering his little bark with the most consummate skill through the vast variety of crafts of various sizes which at that day, before steam almost superseded sailing vessels, lay at anchor in every direction down the Pool. As I paced up and down the deck, occasionally cracking a joke with my kind and facetious friend Tom, my attention was drawn towards the young female before alluded to, who had been addressed by the man now fast asleep on the deck, from whose haggard countenance an admirable sketch might have been taken to depict the hero of Hogarth's "Rake's Progress!" It was no wonder that a lad of seventeen, as I then was, with all the bright visions of life before me, fresh from the society of my joyous companions of old Trinity, should look with interest on this lovely young creature. I saw evidently she was gazing with bewildered look on the wretched object stretched upon the deck, who appeared more like a snoring grampus than a human being. Who could then suppose that he had been an officer of the Royal Marines, a corps from which he had just retired, and had entered upon a career of infamy, moral degradation, and frightful crime, induced by these debasing habits of intemperance and self-indulgence, into which, alas! too many godless and reckless youths are still led by their unbridled passions. Young and innocent-looking as this apparently unfriended girl was, a glance, as it were, of noble indignation flashed across her beautiful countenance, as her black and brilliant eye fixed itself on the mass of living corruption lying prostrate before her. A look of pity mingled with pardonable scorn was visible in every feature, as she beheld the sleeping brute, for the love of whom, as will soon appear, she forsook all the comforts of a dear, though humble home. Here lay the man, to follow whose fortunes she sacrificed adoring parents, loving brothers and sisters, and a devotedly attached uncle, who had adopted her as his own, and who mourned for her as one would for an only child, when he found that she had fled from beneath his roof. To what a state of moral degradation must this wretched man have been reduced, when the very night of the day on which he had led his poor unsuspecting victim to believe that she had become his wife, at the very time when her afflicted relatives were shedding bitter tears over her elopement, by his own confession, expressed in my hearing, and that of every passenger on board, he had been indulging in the grossest revelry and excess! One could almost read her inmost thoughts, as her poor sickening features were gradually withdrawn from the disgusting object still sweltering in a feverish sleep, and with fitful starts and dreaming exclamations already giving an earnest of the dark deeds which he was plotting in his unhallowed mind. "Stephen, ahoi! bring the boat ashore; d———n it, man, I'll blow your brains out if you don't come directly." Then, with clenched hands and teeth, he uttered some horrid imprecations which, though frightful to listen to, gave no definite ideas to those who were witnesses of the scene which I have described, of what was passing in his fiendish thoughts. Leaving this miserable and degraded victim of Satan's wiles to sleep off his late debauchery, I shall reserve for another chapter a conversation which I had with poor Elly, for whose forlorn case I had already begun to feel a deep sympathy.

CHAPTER III.

THE restless slumber of the yet unawakened debauchee had continued, and the evidently unhappy young person whom he addressed when he first came on board (to whose manifest disgust, in common with the great majority of the other passengers, he had described the drunken orgies of the previous night) now sat listlessly musing on the scene which I have described, and seemed racked with the agonizing thoughts which, no doubt, surged in her drooping and afflicted heart. After the lapse of a few minutes, I ventured gently to approach, and having briefly gazed with tender compassion on her lovely countenance, now bedewed with tears, I asked if I could, in any way, be of service to her. Awakened as it were suddenly from a feverish dream, she turned her dark and streaming eyes towards the youth who had politely tendered his devoirs, and had endeavoured, with look and gesture, to inspire with confidence the young female who evidently stood so much in need of consolation. "Pray, young friend," I said, "excuse me for this intrusion, and for thus venturing to address you. I can no longer conceal that I see the cause of your distress; yonder restless sleeper is, no doubt, connected to you by some tie which causes those bitter tears to flow." "Ah, kind sir," she replied, " you have guessed right: That man, that br——— (she suddenly restrained herself, as if a tender thought had curbed her just indignation) is my husband. A few days only have passed since I left my darling uncle's house with him, after pledging his word and honour that he would always love me; and it was but yesterday that the holy Father joined our hands in marriage. Such was the artless, simple, yet true description which was at once confidingly given by this interesting young creature, to one who a few minutes before was a perfect stranger to her. Despairing, as she evidently was, of any sympathy from the man, for whose love she had sacrificed all the blessings and comforts of a happy home, she felt glad that she had found one to whom she might venture to unburthen the load of care which was then crushing her young and guileless heart. How could she respect the vile wretch who the very day after he had led her to believe she was his lawful wife, and had solemnly pledged himself to love and to cherish her, had, as already described, gloried in his shame, in the presence of the company who were now witnesses of his degradation. As soon as I ascertained that I had won her confidence, and felt assured that in her desolate and forlorn condition it was a manifest relief to her to have gained a friend who would sympathize with her in her sorrow, I at once entered into a familiar conversation with her, and learned in a short time the source of that misery, which, in an unguarded moment, she had been led into.

The heartless villain of our tale (who, as before described, was sleeping off the effects of his brutal debauchery) had, while on a sporting excursion, apparently by accident, but with deep design, sought shelter at the humble abode of Elly's uncle, and with the most perfect nonchalance knocked at the cottage door. The shades of night were then gathering around, and as the mansion of an aristocratic friend with whom he was staying on a visit was many miles distant, he made that an excuse to ask for the old man's hospitality, which, with the characteristic generosity of the Irish peasant, was at once freely tendered to him. "Here, Elly dear," cried the venerable and unsuspecting owner of the humble dwelling, "this gentleman who has just knocked at our door seems very wet and cold; sure 'tis hard to think his honour can put up with our poor fare, but we'll give him at all events a 'Cead mille a failtha.'* Put down some turf on

* A hundred thousand welcomes.

the fire, darling; and warm some water for him, and if he'll just sit in the room there for a moment, I'll bring him dry shoes and stockings, which perhaps he will put up with for the present. In a shorter time than I have taken to describe it, this office of kindness was performed, and no sooner had our sportsman thus exchanged his wet hose for a comfortable dry pair, than he threw himself in a lounging attitude into a rustic arm-chair, and enjoyed a cheerful fire, enlivened by native bog deal which might vie with the Yule log of ancient days. The aged host was well supported in his hospitable exertions to provide for all the necessities of the *vanusal;** and while he bustled about to provide a decent spread, little Elly was busy in getting ready a spatchcock and a rasher, and in a miraculously short time a steaming pot of potatoes was prepared to add to the repast, to which their guest now applied himself with a gusto that a London

---

* The Irish for gentleman.

alderman might have envied. While all the master's wants were thus abundantly supplied, his servant Stephen, who sat roasting himself at the hob,* was not neglected, a large plate of bacon and cabbage, with plenty of potatoes, was placed before him, to which, no doubt, he did ample justice. While they were thus discussing the plain but comfortable meal which generous hearts had provided for them, Elly stole quietly away, and having determined to give up her own little bed-room for the night to the *vanusal* who had honoured them with his presence, she placed a pair of snow-white sheets on the couch, and made everything as tidy as circumstances would admit of. When our *gallant hero* had finished his meal, he thanked the kind old man with the most plausible heartiness for the abundant provision he had made for all his wants; and having, with the most winning smiles (which no man was more capable of assuming at pleasure)

---

* The chimney-corner.

paid many elegant compliments to the charming maid who had so gracefully waited upon him, he retired to rest for the night, and was soon buried in a deep sleep.

CHAPTER IV.

When the refreshed sportsman rose in the morning from his comfortable bed, a lily-white cloth was spread, on which was placed some delicious household bread, new-made butter, plenty of fresh eggs, and milk just hot from the cow; which when their guest had partaken of abundantly, he rose to depart, and to renew his sports for another day. During his short stay in this homely, though truly hospitable, abode, he had made a stronger impression on the guileless and innocent heart of poor little Elly than he himself at first was aware of; and though his visit, unconsciously to the inmates, was paid with that intent, he was too well versed in military tactics to assault the fortress at once, but, like a skilful general, he besieged it with the most deep-laid plans, which, unhappily, were too successful. The snipe were so abundant in the neighbourhood of this humble cottage that Mr. S——, of the Royal Marines, during his sojourn at the *Great House** had a good excuse for paying frequent visits to his kind host, whom, after his late warm and hospitable reception, it would of course be the greatest ingratitude to pass by unnoticed. During his numerous calls while in the neighbourhood, he had frequent opportunities, without lying under the slightest suspicion of any sinister object, of conversing with Elly, so, according to the Irish adage, "to make my story short," he at length not only prevailed upon her to elope with him, but capped the climax of his iniquity by the base, mean, and loathsome crime of inducing her to rob her uncle of sixty pounds,† the sum total of his honest earnings for many years; thus committing a rash act which broke the

* The name given by the Irish peasantry to the principal gentleman or squire's residence in the district.

† This fact was related to me by the old man after the murder of his niece.

heart of the venerable old man who loved her as he did his life, ended in her own destruction, and brought the wicked author of all their misery to an ignominious death upon the scaffold.

A very few days after this elopement occurred, the mock marriage, to which I have alluded, took place; and it was, as already stated, the very day after this ceremony was performed that I sailed down the river Shannon with the errant pair, and heard from the lips of the then apparently repenting bride, in her own simple and unadorned language, the substance of the facts I have just related.

Our voyage down the river was very tedious, as the wind was ahead of us, and to this day I have the frequent "ready about"* of the skipper, whenever a tack was to be made, ringing in my ears. I never shall forget the many unavailing attempts which I made to fire at wild fowl (as the old flint lock repeatedly flashed in the pan) with

* An expression used when preparing to tack.

the very gun which was afterwards used as the instrument of poor Elly's destruction. During our tedious passage I had frequent conversations with the almost broken-hearted girl, who was scarcely noticed by her really base seducer, but, as she supposed, her merely careless husband. This wretched man, during the whole time I was on board, when he was not snoring like a grampus upon the deck or in the cabin, was frequently swigging bottles of ale, occasionally mixed with whiskey. I cannot forget the native politeness of poor Elly to myself; she had a well-stored basket of provisions which her vile companion had provided, more, I believe, from selfish motives, as he calculated upon a long day's voyage, than aught he cared for her. This viaticum she freely and delicately offered to share with me, but as my gastronomic powers were sadly out of order from the tossing of the vessel, I merely accepted a little bread and cheese, as I did not wish altogether to decline her kind and well meant offer. Shortly after this her mind evidently began to wander; she talked incessantly to all the passengers, and was quite incoherent in her language. To me, who had heard her history from her own lips, it did not appear so strange, as I knew that her position was most embarrassing; but our fellow voyagers, who were ignorant of the facts, could not conceive the cause of her strange conversation. At one time she used to say that this man, whom we had seen so disgracefully comporting himself, was her husband; at another time, that he was her brother whose mind was astray. Again, she would offer to emigrate to America with any person that would protect her, and pay the passage-money for both. Thus she continued to wander in her speech, and made no secret of her regret for having entrusted herself to the care of the unfeeling savage who never once, that I remember, paid her, during the voyage, the slightest attention.

However disposed one might have been to rescue her from the hands of such a wretch, her own statement that she had married him the night before put interference completely out of the question.*

When the ancient towers of G⸺ Castle came in view, my old friend Tom Mahony hove to, and a boat was immediately at my service to put me on shore. Poor little Elly, who was by no means insensible to the warm interest which I had evinced for her under the sore trial which then weighed down her young, guileless heart, bade me a sad farewell, and looked as if she would gladly, if she were not bound by the ties of matrimony, be delivered from the bondage she was then enduring, and commit herself to the care of some humane person who would restore her to her beloved uncle. As the boat pushed off from the smack, she gave one long and penetrating look, feeling probably, at that sad moment, as if she never again would see, in this dark wilderness of sin, the youth who had listened with such patient and seeming interest to the detail of her late misfortunes.

* It was after the murder it was ascertained that the marriage was a mock one.

She was, however, mistaken in this supposition, as will shortly appear as we proceed with our story.

I was not long in landing on the southern shore of the far-famed river Shannon, close to the ancient gateway of G⸺ Castle, and having asked the porter if the K⸺t was at home, and having been answered in the affirmative, I committed my trunk to the old janitor, who greeted me with a warm "Cead mille a failtha,"* and followed me to the castle where I had been expected for some days. G⸺ Castle was at this period one of the most agreeable mansions in Ireland; its owner was the descendant of an illustrious line of ancestors, and, though he received his education in an English University, was full of Irish frolic and fun, and was a very general favourite in the county, where he held a high position. His wife was one of the loveliest of her sex, and from the hour I had first had the pleasure of being introduced to her to this day on which I write, when widowhood

* Irish for a hundred thousand welcomes.

and many painful trials have traced sorrow on her sweet face, I never experienced anything but the warmest affection from her. Even now, when we talk over the days of my boyhood, when she was in the zenith of full-grown womanly beauty, I take delight to remind her of the affectionate greeting I invariably received at her hands (and which has not ever since one jot abated) when, with joyous and exuberant spirits, I returned for a season to shake off the dust of old *Alma Mater* to enjoy the pleasures of the country.

CHAPTER V.

IMAGINE, gentle reader, a youth of seventeen, who from his earliest boyhood had been trained to all the manly sports of the country, now arrived at the castle of the Knight of G———, whose extensive preserves abounded with game of all sorts; and judge what were his feelings, after having been just released from the restraint of a college life, to have received liberty from the owner of these ancient domains to partake of whatever sport the season would afford. It was now the month of June, and, as the grouse shooting was still full two months off, I had to content myself with hunting hares in the mountains till the challenge of the "Cark a freigh"* on the 20th of August should call

* The Irish for "grouse."

me to the moors, where many of that bold species of the feathered tribe often fell under my skilful hand. When the weather was unfit for out-door sports there were many internal resources in the castle which every guest, according to his taste, might avail himself of. There was an excellent billiard-table in a well lighted room, which furnished a very agreeable pastime for those who were adepts at that interesting game. I am a decided enemy to every sort of gambling; the wretched and demoralizing effects of which I saw abundance of during my college life: but I cannot see why a rational being may not, especially in a private house, amuse himself with a game of billiards as well as with a game of chess. During my sojourn at the castle I often played a game with the K⸺t of G⸺; and we were such equal matches that, after several hours' play, there was scarcely any difference in our scores. The beautiful estuary of the Shannon (which formed a splendid lake-like sheet of water at the foot of the castle lawn, that sloped like a carpet of emerald green to its edge) afforded us many days of wholesome and exhilarating amusement, especially during the summer months, when the K———t frequently planned a pleasure party for his guests, and sailed with them in his yacht to the different points of interest on this noble river. On one of these agreeable trips we visited the town of Kilrush, in the county Clare, where there was a first-rate market for all sorts of provisions, especially a great abundance of excellent fish at a merely nominal price. In those days we frequently purchased a very fine cod-fish for sixpence, and all other kinds at a proportionate rate. An interval of nearly fifty years has made a wonderful difference in the prices of all the articles of life, and though clothing, from the vast improvement in machinery, has been greatly reduced in value, all sorts of butcher's meat and also fish, fowl, and eggs, which are so easily conveyed by railway, have fully doubled in price. The K———t, having left the yacht in care of the skipper, proposed a walk to the town, which was distant about a mile from the fine pier, close to which the vessel was anchored. During our visits to the many excellent shops which abounded in that busy, thriving place, who should greet me with a winning smile and a warm grasp of the hand but dear little Elly, whom a few days before I had left on board the "Lady Frances" packet with him whom she believed was her husband, but who, in fact, was a vile and brutal deceiver. I was truly glad to find her under the protection of my kind old friend Mrs. S——, at whose shop, during my school-boy days, I had often spent my pocket-money in purchasing the delicious fruit with which she was, at the proper seasons, always well supplied. After a brief conversation with my young and interesting friend, and an earnest request to Mrs. S——, for "auld langsyne," to pay her pretty lodger every attention in her power, I bade her (as I then little thought) a last adieu, and quickly rejoined my party, who were hastening to get on board, to take advantage of the flood-tide to waft them back to the castle, which we reached in time for a seven o'clock dinner. While I was thus agreeably spending my vacation, an incident occurred which, though seemingly at first of slight importance, eventually led to the development of one of the foulest conspiracies against human life (unhappily too successful) that ever was recorded in a civilized country.

One day, when the K——t of G—— and I were busily engaged in a well contested game of billiards, there was a sudden summons for the former to visit the town of G—— in his official capacity as a magistrate. At that period of Irish history there was no such thing as a petty sessions court; each magistrate had to act upon his own responsibility. Now, no doubt, as well as then, a sudden emergency may arise, when a gentleman of property and station, who has received the commission of the peace, must act without waiting for the arrival of a second magistrate. Had the case, however, to which I am now about to allude (though, as the result proved, it was pregnant with the most portentous and fearful consequences) occurred in the present day, it would have been dealt with *pro tempore* by the police; and the several parties, who will immediately be brought on the stage, would have been summoned to appear before the magistrates, who would assemble at petty sessions on the next court-day. Had the matter been left altogether to the police, the circumstance which led to the detection of the horrible crime I am about to detail, might never have been noticed. The acute perception, however, of the K——t of G—— (no doubt directed by the wise designs of Providence to bring the guilty to justice) hit upon the first link of that chain of facts which, through the clearest circumstantial evidence, brought conviction to the minds of two enlightened juries.

When the K——t and I had finished our game of billiards, we proceeded together to the town (he in his official capacity as a magistrate, and I as a looker-on) to inquire into the matter he was called upon to investigate. At first view it appeared nothing more than a sort of Billingsgate row between two old women, who were loudly vituperating each other. The subject-matter of their dispute was a cloak, which one of them had pledged with the other, who kept a *Shebeen House*,* for a quart of whiskey as security till she could pay for it in cash. When the purchaser of the liquor subsequently brought the money, and required back the pledge, the seller peremptorily refused to return the article to the owner, who, instead of waiting to recover it by due process of law, determined, *vi et armis*, to have it back then and there. The K——t of G——, accompanied by myself, and with the police in attendance, came upon the disputants, who were evidently preparing for battle, and as tongues were not sufficient to

* An unlicensed house (which abounded in those days) for the sale of intoxicating liquors.

end their strife, were about to try the effects of fisticuffs. The moment, however, they saw the respected and venerated magistrate, " who always dwelt among his own people," and whose word, from his well-known impartiality and even-handed justice, was generally law in that neighbourhood, they immediately desisted and appealed to his decision. On hearing the case he felt it was but just, when the price of the *native* * was tendered, that the pledge should be returned, and therefore directed it to be produced. The proprietor of the *Shebeen House*, though unwilling to part with an article which was vastly more valuable than her whiskey, was constrained to bring it forth. As soon as it was produced the K——t held it out with uplifted arm, asking at the same time where that handsome cloak had come from. Many lovers of dress amongst the crowd that had now assembled looked, no doubt with longing eyes, at the beautiful grey cloth mantle with brilliant green silk hood, wondering

* A popular name for whiskey.

where Mauria S—— could have obtained such a precious garment. While the admiring crowd were gazing in amazement at this article of dress, which was far beyond in its texture a suitable apparel for any of the dames or spinsters who had assembled on this occasion, a woman in the crowd named Ellen W——, who was afterwards the principal witness on the trial, edged stealthily up to the K——t of G—— and whispered a few words into his ear to the following effect, "K——t, I know that cloak; but say no more about it at present." That was quite enough for the active and experienced magistrate; in an instant he took his stand upon what was thus confidentially communicated, and, probably before a single person in that crowd could have observed what had passed between him and Ellen W——, he dismissed the assembly, and was promptly obeyed, as the great body of them had the highest respect for him as a magistrate and a landed proprietor who spent his ample fortune amongst them. Turning to the disputants about the cloak, he said, "I am sure you will have no objection that I should take possession of this article for a few days, after which I shall be sure to return it to the rightful owner." After the crowd had dispersed, and all had proceeded quietly to their several homes, the K——t and I turned our steps towards the castle, chatting on the way respecting this mysterious cloak, quite ignorant at the time of the remarkable events connected with it, and which shortly afterwards were brought to light. After a few hours had elapsed, the K——t sent a confidential messenger to Ellen W——, whom, on her arrival at the castle, he closely questioned. "How did you happen, Ellen," he said, "to know this cloak?" producing the article for her further inspection. "I saw it, K——t," she replied, "on Mrs. S——," (meaning Ellen Hanly, who, in consequence of the general supposition that she had been married to Lieutenant S——, went by that name). K——t: "Where did you see her wear it?" Ellen W——: "In several places since her marriage, for I acted for some time as her waiting maid." K——t: "Where is Mrs. S—— now?" Ellen W——: "That I cannot tell; the last place I saw her was at Carrig Island, near Ballylongford, where I was dismissed, as Lieutenant S—— told me he was going to take her home for a short time to her uncle's." K——t: "Do you think she is there now?" Ellen W——: "Indeed, K——t, I fear she is not, for bad stories are going about, and when I saw the cloak this morning, and particularly when it was claimed by Mauria S——, who is sister to Stephen S——, Lieutenant S——'s boatman (as bad a boy as any from this to Cork), I trembled in my skin, and my knees shook under me; oh, K——t, asthore!* from the way lately that Lieutenant S—— and Stephen his boatman *thrated* the poor darling crathur in my presence, there was nothing too bad for them to do." While this questioning and answering was proceeding, a tapping was heard at the library door, which

* Irish for "My dear."

was immediately opened by the K——t, who, having asked the cause, was told by the servant that a party of police were at the hall door, urgently requesting to see him with the least possible delay. What followed this interruption, I shall relate in another chapter.

CHAPTER VI.

THE K——t, having told Ellen W—— to remain seated, attended at once to the summons which he had received, and, as he made no objection that I should be a witness to his conference with the constables, I accompanied him to the hall door, where they were waiting. "Well, Sergeant F——," said the K——t, "what is the matter now? Has this row between those hags recommenced?" "No, K——t," said the chief constable, "but an express from the county Clare has just arrived, stating that the dead body of a female has been cast ashore between this and Kilrush, very near Money Point, and strong suspicion exists that there has been foul play." "From what occurred this morning about the cloak," said the sergeant, "it struck me that there might be some connexion between the events, and I therefore felt it my duty to inform your worship of the fact, in order that you might act as you thought fit." The K——t, with his usual promptness in action, at once formed his resolution, and sent immediate orders to his skipper, Jack M——, to prepare the yacht without delay for a sail down the river. He, at the same time, ordered the sergeant to get a party of his men under arms with the utmost possible despatch, and to be ready to accompany him in the vessel. As soon as the police left the castle to execute the orders they had received, the K——t again addressed himself to Ellen W—— and said, " Depend upon it, Ellen, that those 'bad stories,' which a few minutes ago you said were going about, will find their true solution in the terrible revelation which is now about to manifest itself in connexion with the subject of our conversation. How strange that this seemingly insignificant fact of a row between two old hags should so soon be brought to bear upon this case, which it is my imperative duty to investigate! How fortunate for the ends of justice that you, unconscious when you joined that crowd this morning of what was about to take place, should now be able to give a clue to the discovery of what I fear has been committed, the foul and brutal murder of this poor young woman, upon whom, you tell me, you attended for several days. Get ready at once, Ellen, as I mean to take you with me in the yacht; and I promise you that, if you will only determine to tell the truth, and, without fear of consequences, reveal all you know about the matter, you shall receive every protection which it is in my power to give, and, exclusive of the satisfaction you will feel in your own conscience from being an instrument in the hands of Providence of bringing to light a horrible deed of darkness, your country will applaud you for being an honest and willing witness in perhaps discovering the foul perpetrator of what, I fear, will turn out to be a horrid murder." The K——t, after thus judiciously addressing himself to Ellen W——, turned to me and said, "R——d, I know you are fond of a sail, and also deal a little in the romantic; get ready therefore, my boy, in a jiffy, and accompany me in the yacht." While the conference which I have just related was proceeding, I can scarcely describe the dreadful thoughts that were passing through my mind. From all Ellen W—— had said, I feared that the young woman, upon whom she had attended, was identical with Elly, whose history I had heard from herself on board the packet, and that the female whose remains were reported as cast ashore near Money Point, in the county Clare, was the same ill-fated, poor creature. It was no time, however, to delay reflecting on this sad catastrophe, therefore, as the K——t had invited me to accompany him, I ran up-stairs to my dressing-room, quickly donned my yachting dress, and was soon ready for the excursion. The only difficulty at this moment which seemed to present itself, and was likely to cause some delay, was the absence of one of the yacht's regular hands, but this want was soon supplied in the person of Jack K——, a very civil, experienced sailor, who happened to be present on the wharf. The K——t thus addressed the man alluded to, "Jack, my friend, Bill M—— is away, and as I am in a hurry to take advantage of the falling tide, to run down the river towards Money Point, will you, like an honest fellow, bear a hand with us?" "With a thousand welcomes, K——t," replied Jack, "I would go up to my neck in the *say* to oblige your honour." No sooner said than done; honest Jack at once took the place assigned to him, and assisted with alacrity the other men to prepare for the start. The sequel will show how singular it was, and how necessary to the ends of justice, that *this* man should have been on the spot at the very time his assistance was wanted. We all now jumped on board, and before many minutes had elapsed, were running with a favourable tide and a rattling breeze towards Money Point, near which, it was reported to the K——t, that, the dead body of a female had been thrown on shore. As soon as we reached the place, we saw a man walking on the beach, and having asked if he had heard anything about the matter in question, he turned out to be the identical person who found the dead body the day before, and had buried it in the sand. The K——t immediately asked if there was any gentleman living close to the place? and he replied that there was, pointing to the residence of Mr. F——, a gentleman of property in the neighbourhood. The K——t further inquired if Mr. F—— was aware that a dead body had been cast upon the shore? to which the man replied, that he certainly was, as he had seen the corpse himself. The K——t then asked him if Mr. F—— had reported the circumstance to Major W——, the very efficient head of the police, who resided at Kilrush, about three miles from the spot? He replied, he did not think he had, as no police party had visited the place since he found the mutilated remains, which, on being questioned as to the sex, he stated he could distinctly swear were those of a female. Without further delay, he took us to the spot where he had buried the body in the sand, within a short distance of the landing place. When we reached the grave we beheld the horrifying spectacle of a human leg protruding from the sand, and in consequence of the decomposing remains being so near the surface, an almost intolerable stench filled the air around us. The next step which the K——t of G—— took, was to despatch a messenger to Kilrush for Major W—— and the police, and as no coroner was to be had within any reasonable distance, the K——t determined that he and his brother magistrate last named should, on his arrival, hold an inquest, which it was quite lawful for them to do. Little more than an hour had elapsed after the departure of the express messenger, when Major W——, on horseback, and a strong escort of mounted police made their appearance. Having warmly greeted his old friend the K——t of G——, and heartily shaken hands with me, who had enjoyed his hospitality, and joined in the sports of his children during my school-boy days at Kilrush, he asked the cause of this urgent summons. The dreadful spectacle which was close at hand was pointed out to him, immediately after which the K——t and he had some private conversation preparatory to the exhuming of the body. The next step which was taken was to impannel a jury, which was no difficult task, as the rapid progress of the police force from Kilrush, had quickly drawn a crowd to the spot, from amongst whom the jury was speedily selected. I never can forget the circumstances attending the raising of the body from its shallow grave on the beach, to be viewed by the magistrates and the jury before proceeding on the business of the inquest. The stench of the putrifying remains, which must have been bereft of life several weeks, was so dreadful, that the police had to keep up a constant explosion of gunpowder to deaden its offensive effects, and to give the jury and the witnesses an opportunity of examining it. Ellen W——, the witness, for reasons which will just now appear, was not as yet allowed to see the body, and was therefore removed to some distance from the spot. When the body was raised from the sand in which it was so imperfectly buried, it was found that one of the legs was missing, while the other was tied to the neck with a rope; and now mark, reader, the singular bearings of this latter fact. When we started from the quay at G——, it seemed to be a mere matter of accident that Jack K—— should have taken a hand with us in the yacht, but no sooner did he see the rope just alluded to than he exclaimed "*I know that rope.*" The Book was immediately handed to him by Major W——; he was sworn on the Holy Volume, and deposed as follows: " I met Lieutenant S—— and his man, Stephen S——, in

G——, about six or seven weeks ago, when the former asked me for the loan of a rope, as he was going to take a sail in his boat, and I lent one to him; I swear positively that the rope now in my hand is the *same*." Major W——: "How do you know that it is?" "I'd swear to my own splicing in any part of the world, and it was my own two hands that joined these two pieces together;" pointing at the same time distinctly to the joining, which, notwithstanding its long immersion in water, was quite perfect. This testimony from a man who, exclusive of the blunt, honest, straightforward character which he had preserved unblemished (I trust I may say to the present day, for he is still alive), coupled with his intimate acquaintance with the parties who were suspected of this foul murder, had great weight with the jury, and left no doubt on their minds of the guilt of these wretched men. All who were present expressed quietly to each other, without at all interrupting the progress of the inquest, their amazement at the chain of circumstantial evidence which was every moment throwing light upon this horrid conspiracy against the life of this young and guileless victim. There was, however, one very necessary link in the chain which was yet wanted, and was of the utmost importance, if possible, to have supplied,— namely, the identity of the dead, and, no doubt, murdered female, then lying a mangled and ghastly corpse before us, with Ellen Hanley, who for several weeks had been missing from her uncle's house. I had previously remarked that Ellen W——, the witness who had accompanied us in the yacht, had not as yet seen the body. My reader will recollect that the man who first found it on the shore swore that it was the body of a female; the skull, however, was so completely bereft of hair and flesh that it was utterly impossible for the nearest and dearest friend of poor Ellen Hanley, by merely looking at that bleached member of the human frame, to say that the body was hers. The magistrates took Ellen W—— aside, and produced for her examination a stays (which is also called a bodice) which was taken from the remains, and asked her if she thought she could distinctly swear to that article. The reason they put this question to her was, because she had previously stated that while acting in the capacity of her maid-servant, she had frequently laced her stays: she looked intently at this article of dress, and though she said she could almost be certain that it was the very one she had so often handled, she honestly refused, when the lives of her fellow-creatures might hang upon her declaration, to swear positively to it, and assigned as a reason for not doing so that it would not be safe, considering the rotten state it was in, absolutely to say it was the same. The magistrates and the jury, though, in other respects, perfectly convinced that it *was* the body of Ellen Hanly (who had not been seen for several weeks and could not be traced) which lay before them, determined, in order to work out perfectly the ends of justice, to leave no stone unturned, if possible, to prove beyond all reasonable doubt, that it was the identical body of this poor girl. When every effort seemed almost hopeless, and when Ellen W—— had been questioned and cross-questioned, her reply always was, "If I saw her darling face I would know her at once." This we all felt was impossible, as, alas! no face was there: therefore, being hopeless of legally proving the identity by this witness, we were just about to gratify her with viewing the remains, which none of us had any reasonable doubt were those of poor Elly, when, by a sudden and unaccountable impulse, I laid my hand upon her shoulder, addressing her at the same time in rather a startling manner thus, "*Think of yourself, Ellen!** perhaps you may recollect something that could make it clear to the jury, beyond all question, that the body you are now about to see is that of Ellen Hanly. The words had scarcely escaped my lips, when, as if inspired by some immediate

* A very common mode of speech in Ireland.

revelation, she loudly exclaimed, "Oh sir, yes, yes, I remember now she had two double teeth in her upper jaw (placing her fingers at the same time on her own mouth, thus suiting the action to the word), and though you tell me her sweet face is gone, I could show the very spots where those white teeth, I so often saw, were placed. No sooner had she made this statement than the skull was closely examined; the teeth had disappeared, but the double sockets remained, identically as she had described them. The body was then exposed to the view of Ellen W——; on beholding which she burst into a flood of tears, and as soon as she had somewhat recovered her equanimity, she placed her fingers on the sockets, and swore distinctly that, as far as human judgment could go, such were the identical receptacles of the once lovely teeth of that young and interesting creature. This evidence completely satisfied the jury as to the identity of the body, which they declared to be that of Ellen Hanly, who had, they were convinced, been murdered about six weeks before, and their verdict was, that Lieutenant John S—— and Stephen S—— were guilty of that foul crime. Now that the verdict had been returned, and the magistrates had had a short consultation, they both declared that they not only felt it their bounden duty to state that they perfectly concurred in the result of the inquest, but that they could not separate without pronouncing their marked displeasure respecting the conduct of the neighbouring resident gentleman, who, from what the man who found the body thrown in upon the shore, had stated, was perfectly cognizant of the fact, and yet had allowed it to lie for twenty-four hours in its shallow and ill-made grave, without reporting the matter to Major W—— at Kilrush. Were any public functionary in the present day guilty of such a manifest dereliction of duty, he would no doubt, without much ceremony, be dismissed from his office, and were a private gentleman of the same station as Mr. ——, who resided within a few hundred yards of Elly's grave, to leave so serious a matter unnoticed for a whole day, he would, no doubt, be severely censured in the public press, and would incur the marked disapprobation of his compeers, and of every lover of order. The important business of the inquest having now closed, and the piece of rope, which in such a remarkable manner had been identified and sworn to by Jack K——, having been marked by himself with a blue thread, preparations were made for the decent interment of the body in the next church-yard, until her friends could be communicated with: and it was accordingly followed to the grave, which was close at hand, by all the party who had witnessed the solemn ceremonial of the inquest, and many a salt tear, on that mournful occasion, bedewed the cold earth which was laid upon the mangled remains of her who had fallen a victim, in the bloom of youth, to the lust and cupidity of a fiend in human shape. This monster of iniquity was, as before stated, an officer in his Majesty's service,* who, instead of upholding the honour and dignity of the noble defenders of our country, was now to be hunted down as a degraded felon, who was accused of one of the foulest crimes that had ever blackened the pages of its history.

Here I would diverge from my narrative, in order briefly to address my reader on a subject which I fervently pray may arrest his serious attention. My heartfelt appeal is specially intended for the young and inexperienced of every class in life, including that honourable profession to which John S—— was a disgrace. The great body of them would, I am convinced, die a thousand deaths ere they would quail before the foe, but alas! is it not too true that many of those engaged in their country's service rend the hearts of their parents, who have frequently many domestic difficulties to contend with, by the reckless extravagance in which they too often indulge, and thus bring ruin upon themselves and the

* The murder took place in the reign of George III.

guardians of their youth? I would earnestly conjure such to look on this picture of real life, which I have endeavoured, without the slightest exaggeration, faithfully to sketch. I have recorded simple facts from personal experience, and a memory from which nothing but second childhood can ever efface this fearful tragedy. Oh! may none whom I address, who are exposed to similar temptations, which led the wretched malefactor here brought before them to an untimely death upon the scaffold, be highminded, but fear: lest the enemy of souls should use the same engines to entrap them, and lead them to destruction and perdition. Here is the young man of good position, and, for aught I know to the contrary, possessing adequate means in addition to his pay, to secure him every reasonable comfort; the scion of an ancient family, and connected with some of the best blood in the country, a youth of high and aspiring promise, of noble mien, belonging to an honourable and gallant profession, giving way to his corrupt passions, and without the slightest compunction, not only bringing disgrace and ruin upon a poor young female far below his rank in life, but with mean and low cupidity inducing her to rob an affectionate relative of his all, to minister to his own ungodly vices! A few days sufficed to show him the dark side of the picture which he had painted for himself. He felt acutely how unequally he was yoked, and what a ferment it would create in the aristocratic families with which he was connected, to hear of the union he had formed. He knew full well that the marriage was only a sham, and yet instead, on cool reflection, of trying by legitimate means to repair the damage he had done, he makes a short cut to the solution of the difficulty he was placed in, by conspiring against the life of his victim, and so removing her out of his way. Here surely is a warning, an awful warning, to thoughtless youth, against giving way to wicked passions, and a solemn call to those who are exposed to similar temptations, to pray for that grace of

God which can alone preserve them from the snares of the arch-enemy of their souls. Having thus briefly endeavoured to warn my young readers of this story of real life, I shall recur, in the following chapter, to the circumstances which immediately followed the delivery of the verdict.

CHAPTER VII.

The K——t of G——, who took such prompt and active measures to trace out and arrest the perpetrators of this horrible crime, had, during the progress of the inquest, received information that Lieutenant S——, who had just been pronounced guilty by the coroner's jury, was lurking somewhere in the neighbourhood, determined at once to use every exertion in his power to have him arrested. We were now on the Clare side of the river, and the K——t's residence was several miles up, towards Limerick, on the opposite bank. As he knew he could not, by possibility, return home that night without giving up the pursuit, and fearing that his young and beautiful wife might feel uneasy at his absence, without receiving intimation of the cause of it, he addressed me thus: "R——d, will you have the kindness to return at once to G—— Castle in the yacht, and tell B——t that I have felt myself called upon, after the dreadful revelations which have come to my knowledge since I saw her this morning, to endeavour to arrest the villains, who no doubt are the perpetrators of this shocking crime, and I have strong reason to believe that one of them is not far off from where we are now standing. To-morrow morning come yourself, if you can, or at all events send the yacht to meet me at Cahercon, when I hope to be able to report the capture of one or both of the murderers of this poor young woman." After some further conversation, I got the vessel under weigh, and in about an hour's sail up the river, reached the beautiful baronial mansion of my kinsman, where I found the family on the tiptoe of expectation, and anxious to know the result of the excursion which was so hurriedly undertaken in the early part of that day. Having given them a brief descrip-

‑tion of the leading circumstances of the inquest, and having stated who the persons were against whom the verdict had been pronounced, all were struck with amazement when they learned that an officer, who was connected with some of the first families in the county, was declared guilty (with scarcely a shadow of a doubt) of the fearful crime of murder. After the exertion and excitement of that long and eventful day, and having partaken of the hospitality of G—— Castle, I was truly glad to seek repose, as I had again to leave at an early hour the next morning to rejoin the K——t of G—— at the rendezvous he had appointed. Having enjoyed a comfortable and refreshing slumber, I took a hasty breakfast, and was soon skimming over the waters of the beautiful Shannon, and ere long reached Cahercon where, with his usual punctuality, I found the K——t of G—— waiting for me. "Well, R——d," he said, addressing me, "I have not been so successful as I had hoped; the villain S—— has escaped me for the present.

Had I been an hour sooner on his track, you would, more than probable, have seen him now in the hands of justice. I have, however, made such arrangements that I think it scarcely possible he can escape much longer, and I shall be greatly disappointed if at next assizes he does not plead, before God and his country, respecting the atrocious crime with which he and Stephen S——, his companion in guilt, stand charged. Notwithstanding all the exertions that this active and unwearied magistrate could make, and every plan which the authorities and police force (which in consequence of the disturbances that then prevailed was very large) could devise, no trace could be had of the hiding-place of Lieutenant S——, who, it was almost certain, was still in the country; but it was generally believed that his man, Stephen S——, had escaped to America. A very decided impression had got abroad that several influential persons in the county, with whom the wretched criminal was closely connected, had helped to screen him from justice, hoping that means could be adopted to convey him to some distant land. With, however, these few exceptions, almost every man's hand throughout the country was against him, and after many unsuccessful searches, he was at length arrested where it would have been least expected that he would venture to lie hid. My recollection of the capture is as follows: reliable information having been received that Lieutenant S—— had been several times seen lurking about his father's house, Mr. T—— S—— R——, an influential magistrate, heir to a large fortune in the county, accompanied by a troop of lancers and a large police force, surrounded the mansion. Every room in the house and every out-office was diligently searched, and not a corner where a human being could be concealed escaped the scrutinizing eyes of the large force which had been disposed throughout the premises, with the most consummate skill, by the civil and military officers; still no capture had been effected. Just, however, as orders had been given to the troops and the police to retire, one of the lancers made a lunge of his weapon through a heap of straw which, by some means, had been passed over, when the wretched criminal, who narrowly escaped being run through, as the lance grazed his skin, suddenly sprang from his hiding-place, and with eye-balls staring from his haggard face, cried out with agonizing shrieks for mercy. Short work was now made of the matter: The no doubt guilty wretch was at once taken into custody, his wrists bound together with handcuffs; and amidst the cries and tears of his broken-hearted family, was taken off to the county jail. As the proofs of his guilt were all circumstantial, great care was taken by the legal authorities that not a link should be wanting to complete the case. The very able functionaries, whose skill and acuteness in sifting evidence in these eventful times (when "Captain Rock" and his troops were doing all in their power to unloose the bands of society) had unfortunately too often to be tried, determined, as far as in them lay, to leave nothing to mere conjecture, and, when putting the unhappy accused on his trial, resolved to bring the matter in such a way before the court and jury as would thoroughly convince them of his guilt. While I leave the wretched prisoner, after his arrest and subsequent committal, to reflect upon the terrible position in which he was placed (a position which would no doubt have been fearful in the extreme to the humblest peasant in the land, but unquestionably far more so to one who was born of gentle parents, and was brought up with every comfort, if not in the lap of luxury), I shall briefly relate an incident that I witnessed myself, which was so touching in its nature, and so truly pathetic in its bearing, that it indelibly fixed itself in my memory.

Shortly after the discovery of the body of poor Elly, the conclusion of the coroner's inquest, as already related, and the consigning of her mutilated remains to the grave, I was one morning with the K——t of G—— in his dressing-room, a short time before breakfast. While we were chatting together about the events of that remarkable period of Ireland's history, the room-door was suddenly thrown open, when two countrymen rushed in (rather, as the reader may judge, an alarming sort of visit in those perilous times), and at once prostrated themselves with their faces to the ground, at the same time exhibiting signs of the deepest and most agonizing grief, and crying out in language which would have touched the most obdurate heart, " Oh! K——t, K——t, if we could only see her, alive or dead!!—Oh! if we could but see her darling face once more!!!" These poor, seemingly almost broken-hearted men, were the father and uncle of the murdered Elly. Having long searched in vain to discover the whereabouts of their lost, ruined, and deceived child, they at length received tidings of the finding of her murdered remains, and having heard of the active part which the K——t of G—— took in the whole transaction, they thus unceremoniously rushed into his presence, and though startling at the moment this early visit was to him and me, when we learned the real state of the case, we readily did all in our power to comfort the poor afflicted ones, and promised, as far as practicable, that their wishes should be gratified in seeing the body of their poor child, which of course they should have liberty to do, if they should think fit to raise it from its then resting-place.

The time of trial now approached, and everything that rank and influence (if not for the sake of the miserable prisoner, in order if possible to avoid the stigma which they supposed would attach to his relatives, some of whom were of noble blood) could do to secure an acquittal was actively resorted to. The magistrates, at the same time, who sifted the whole matter from the beginning, and were so well acquainted with the facts that they entertained no reasonable doubt of the prisoner's guilt, gave their untiring assistance to the able and experienced Crown solicitor of that day, who had the most talented counsel the Government could retain to assist him in preparing for investigation this remarkable case, which, it was expected, would bring to light such deeds of atrocity as were seldom laid before a criminal court. All the pomp and circumstance which usually attend the arrival of the judges of assize was carried out to the full, and curiosity was wrought up to the highest pitch of excitement when it was known that the trial of an officer and a gentleman of high birth, for one of the greatest crimes known to the law, the crime of murder, was to take place. The Honourable R—— J——, fourth justice of the King's Bench, and the Honourable H—— J——, first sergeant, took their appointed seats. Amid the deep silence of one of the most crowded courts that ever was known in the city, the prisoner was put forward, and with firm, unflinching step he walked to the bar, which he clutched with apparently an iron grasp, and when arraigned as the murderer of Ellen Hanly, *alias* S——n, to the usual question "Are you guilty or not guilty?" he responded, in a clear and rather musical voice, "Not guilty." The trial then proceeded. The several witnesses, before alluded to, were closely examined and cross-examined, and the counsel for the Crown, while they faithfully did their duty, gave every facility to the counsel for the defence to sift the credibility of the witnesses by all the ingenuity they could command, so as, if possible, to cast doubt upon their testimony, and to break the circumstantial chain, which, in order to secure a conviction, it was necessary to preserve indissoluble. In this the Crown prosecutors perfectly succeeded, for though for the defence an amount of talent was extemporized on that occasion from the powerful bar which was on circuit such as no ordinary prisoner could possibly command, the several links of evidence were so firmly welded together, that no human energy could break them, and after as patient and searching a trial as ever took place in that court, the terrible verdict of "*guilty*" was brought in, and I have now before me an exact and veritable copy of the court document, which is couched in the following words: "Verdict, *Guilty*—to be hanged by the neck until dead, on Thursday the 16th of March instant, and his body to be given to the surgeons of the County Limerick Infirmary to be dissected and anatomized. True Bill 64—John S—— committed by the Mayor, 14th November 1819. Judgment and for murder of Ellen Hanly on 4th of July 1819. True Bill—Stephen S——*, *extra*." No sooner was the wretched prisoner convicted, no doubt with the decided approval of every one in that court (his own immediate friends and relatives excepted), than the senior judge, with slow and solemn movement, placed on his head the black cap, at that time the emblem of certain death, and then pronounced, in a clear and distinct voice, the fearful sentence of the law awarded to a capital crime. "John S——, you shall be removed from the place where you stand

* The accused, Stephen S——, was not yet arrested.

to the jail, and from thence to the common place of execution, where you shall be hanged by the neck until you are dead, and your body given to the surgeons for dissection. And may the Lord have mercy upon your soul!" While this dread ordeal was passing, not a muscle seemed to move in the countenance of the wretched convict. Not even the presence of his unhappy relatives (many of whom were in court, under the almost certain conviction when they entered it that he must be acquitted) could in the slightest degree affect the firm demeanour he assumed, which they attributed to conscious innocence, but which was no doubt (as the sequel proved) the result of hardened guilt. There he stood, unmoved and apparently unappalled, during the few moments which elapsed between his sentence and his removal to the condemned cell, which he would never leave till the morning upon which he would be launched into eternity. Within five days from the time he was arraigned he was brought forth for execution, and as the jails were not at that time provided with those drops, on which many a convicted criminal has since that day expiated his crimes, he was taken to Gallows Green, under the gaze of an immense multitude, who, with quiet and becoming demeanour, assented to the justice of his sentence. He was allowed the privilege of a carriage to convey him to the place of execution, and it was only after the greatest exertions on the part of his friends that such a vehicle could be procured. They had scarcely started from the jail when the horses sulked, and though, in addition to the repeated lashing of the driver, the soldiers used their bayonets and prodded the restive animals to force them onwards, they determinately revolted against all their efforts, and would not move an inch towards the fatal spot. The convict himself, seeing no chance of a forward movement, sprung alertly from the carriage, and walked with firm and undaunted step towards the place of execution. This resolute manifestation of unshaken courage, under the dreadful circumstances in which he was placed, led several of the uneducated and credulous spectators to assert that he was innocent, and that the horses instinctively refused to participate in the death of a guiltless man; and they were loud in their exclamations of pity. The law, however, which condemned him, should take its course, as all the efforts of his friends to obtain a respite were fruitless. When he reached the fatal spot where he was to expiate the crime of which he had been convicted, and when the executioner had pinioned him, and gone through all the preliminaries of his too often necessary, yet horrid, office, he drew the white cap over his face, and having placed him standing on the cart, which was a substitute for a drop, he was just about to launch him into eternity when the sheriff stayed his hand, and directed him to remove the cap which he had put on him. He then addressed the wretched convict in words to the following effect: "Mr. S——, you are to appear in a few moments before the awful throne of your Creator. You have been convicted of the dreadful crime of which you stood charged, after as patient and searching a trial as ever was given to man. A jury of twelve honest, upright, impartial gentlemen, of the class in life which you might have adorned, have pronounced you guilty, of the righteousness of which verdict neither the humane and upright judges who tried you, or the overwhelming majority of those who heard the trial, have any reasonable doubt. It would therefore be a satisfaction to all, and would in some measure lessen the atrocity of your guilt, if you would make a full confession now, while life remains. Do not, I entreat you, suppose that in my thus addressing you, you have the slightest chance of a reprieve. I pledge myself to you, as a man of honour, that I have no authority to hold out any hope, as I believe in my conscience that your doom is inevitably sealed." Notwithstanding this solemn and earnest address of the sheriff, the wretched convict, who had been offered this last opportunity of acknowledging the justness of his sentence (as we shall hereafter see was such as his fearful crime deserved), thus replied: "I thought a few minutes ago that I should never see the light of heaven again! May the gates of Paradise be for ever shut against me if I had hand, act or part, in the crime for which I am now about to suffer!" Scarcely were these words expressed, when, at the signal of the Sheriff, the cap was placed again over his eyes by the executioner, the rope was adjusted, a lash was given to the horse which was attached to the cart, and the miserable culprit was launched into eternity.

We shall now let the curtain drop over so much of this sad and real tragedy, which memory recalls with the most vivid and painful recollections, of as shocking a picture of human depravity as ever was recorded, and shall reserve for another chapter some facts connected with the arrest, trial, conviction, and final confession of Stephen S——, the other culprit charged as being the aider and abettor of John S—— in this cruel murder.

CHAPTER VIII.

After the execution of John S—— (which the general voice of the public, and the great majority of the nobility and gentry of the county, felt and declared to be fit and right) a considerable number of the friends and relatives of the culprit strongly asserted that it was a judicial murder, and vented the bitterness they no doubt (perhaps pardonably) felt, in loud exclamations of condemnation against all who had taken an active part in tracing out the murderer and bringing him to justice, especially against my friend the K——t of G——.

About six months had passed away since John S—— had expiated his foul crime by an ignominious and terrible death, and notwithstanding the most strenuous exertions to capture, or gain information about, Stephen S——, no clue could be got to come upon his track. One of my brothers and myself were staying at that time on a visit with a friend in Tralee, the county town of Kerry. A man had been arrested in the small town of Castleisland, about eight miles from Tralee, upon (as well as I recollect) the charge of having absconded with a sum of money with which he had been entrusted by his father-in-law, a tithe-proctor. That class of men, in those by-gone days of which I speak, were of rather questionable repute, and were looked upon by the masses of the people, by reason of their grinding exactions (of which I fear they were too often guilty), in much the same light as the publicans of old were esteemed by the majority of the Jewish people. Very little sympathy was therefore felt for "*the ould Jew,*" as they called him, and they pronounced the act of his son-in-law in having fleeced him, as rather praiseworthy than otherwise, because, as they asserted, he withheld the portion which he had promised his daughter at her marriage; and it was therefore no harm, according to their mode of reasoning, to spoil the *ould Egyptian*. Little did those legislators (who, however wrongheaded and impulsive they too often are, nevertheless exhibit frequently a good deal of rude justice in the conclusions they came to) know who the man was that they were endeavouring to justify for robbing old Moses. Shortly after the arrest alluded to, a gentleman who had been making a tour through the country, and had been inspecting the several public institutions (the county jail of Kerry amongst them), having read in the *Hue and Cry* a description of Stephen S——, who stood charged as an accomplice of John S—— in the murder of Ellen Hanly, in going through the different wards of the prison, strongly suspected that he saw amongst the prisoners a man agreeing thereto. He at once communicated his suspicions to the jailor, who, as soon as his attention had been drawn to the matter, and having closely inspected the man alluded to, agreed with the visitor that there was strong ground for supposing that he might be the person who stood charged with this dreadful murder. By some means or other it reached the ears of the authorities that my brother and I were in town, and as we were residents of the county Limerick, close to the town of G——; the native place of Stephen S——, it was thought that we might be able to identify him, if it really was he that was now in the jail. A polite message was sent to us by the sheriff requesting that, as soon as we conveniently could, we would take a walk to the prison and look through the different wards, and in case we should recognise Stephen S—— would be good enough to say so. When such a criminal was looked after we could, of course, offer no reasonable objection to the request, and accordingly about ten o'clock next morning we repaired to the county jail. On our arrival, the sheriff, accompanied by the governor, conducted us through the different wards, in each of which a good many prisoners were assembled. Having stopped for a few minutes in one of the rooms, I was particularly struck with the demeanour of a prisoner who attracted my attention by the remarkable change of countenance which he manifested when his eye caught mine. He was smoking, seemingly in the most unconcerned manner, when I first saw him, and as he was a particularly athletic, tall, and by no means repulsive looking man, I fixed my eye steadily upon him, without any particular thought just then that he was the suspected person. Suddenly the pipe fell from his mouth; he hung down his head, and evidently averted his countenance from the direction where I was standing. It was only then that I remarked to the governor of the jail, who was standing near me, " See how my presence affects that man; I can't say that he is Stephen S——, as I have never known him by that name, but he surely knows me, and I should not be surprised if that is the very man you are looking after." The governor replied, " Yes,

Sir, that is the man that *is* thought to be Stephen S——, but as you don't know him to be such, we must try and have him identified by some person who is acquainted with his person." That very day a messenger was despatched to G——, in the county Limerick, his native place; and J—— C——, a constable in the town who knew him well, was sent for, who the moment he saw him went up to him, shook hands with him, and said, "How do you do, Stephen S——?" As soon as this interview took place he acknowledged himself to be the man that was accused of the murder of Ellen Hanly; but in a very firm and decided manner denied his guilt. A warrant was made out, under which he was transmitted, accompanied by a strong escort of dragoons, to the county Limerick jail. He remained in custody, in that prison, till the summer assizes 1820, when he was arraigned before the Right Honourable C—— K—— B——, and Honourable H—— J——, first sergeant, on the 21st July, and convicted on the evidence of the same witnesses (one or two excepted) that were examined on the trial of John S——, and I have now the verdict before me. " Tuesday—Verdict, *Guilty :* Stephen S—— hanged by the neck until dead at the common place of execution, and his body to be given to the surgeons of the County Limerick Infirmary for dissection, on Thursday, 27th of July instant. True Bill No. 1. Stephen S—— committed on transmit warrant from county Kerry, 17th June 1820." Immediately after the conviction of the wretched man, he, without hesitation, confessed his guilt, expressing at the same time a wish to unburden his mind and to reveal the whole circumstances connected with this most atrocious murder, in the presence of the magistrates and gentlemen of the county. Previous to this *denouement* having taken place, it was very currently reported that some influential friends of the executed convict John S——, who were magistrates of the county, and as such had free access to the jail, paid a visit to the condemned criminal in his cell, and asked him to declare the innocence of John S——, who had been, as they asserted, innocently hanged. This he positively refused to do, stating, at the same time, that though John S—— was not the actual murderer, it was he that plotted the whole thing, and forced him, while in a fit of drunkenness, to perpetrate the crime. The facts connected with this fearful tragedy he thus related, and declared as a dying man that they were strictly correct. He first corroborated everything that Ellen W——, the principal witness, had related to the K——t of G——, and swore to on both trials, and acknowledged that he had, under disguise, personated a Roman Catholic clergyman, when he celebrated the marriage between John S—— and Ellen Hanly. He further stated that he and John S——, in order to ensure the sinking of the body, as soon as the murder should take place, and that there should be no danger of its ever rising to the surface of the water (which it afterwards did, bringing home guilt to the unmerciful perpetrators), had provided a large stone, of a couple of hundredweight, in which they sunk an iron staple, which they leaded firmly into it, attaching thereto an iron chain, to which they intended to fasten the body previous to consigning it to the deep. When all was prepared for action, by a preconcerted arrangement between them, Stephen S—— was to come down in the boat from G—— to Carrig Island where John S—— and Elly were spending the honeymoon, and under the pretext of a pleasure-excursion to a neighbouring island in the river Shannon, where there were some remarkable monuments of antiquity, these two atrocious villains had planned, when they should reach the middle of the widest part of this great river, where no human eye could be upon them, to beat the brains out of their victim, and then attach her murdered body to the stone which they had prepared, and sink it in mid-channel, never, as they hoped, again to be seen. In pursuance of this plan they launched off on their excursion towards the island before alluded to, poor Elly in the highest delight, with the anticipation of seeing the venerated image of Saint Sennanus (of whom she had often heard) and of worshipping at his shrine. When they had reached mid-channel John S—— made to Stephen S—— the preconcerted signal, at which the work of death was to commence, but the wretched villain, though hardened enough before for any deed of wickedness, seemed to take no notice of the repeated signs which he made. At length, after various attempts to gain his attention, he drew up close to him, and in a whisper asked him what he was about. Stephen S—— quietly answered, in a low voice, that when he looked upon her sweet, innocent face he could not bring himself to hurt a hair of her head; and when John S—— still urged him to assist in the dreadful act, he gave him a very broad hint, that if he attempted any violence, he would pitch him overboard, which, being a very athletic man, he could easily have done. John S——, seeing it was useless to urge the matter further, on some pretext or other, such as the weather looking lowering, and the day likely to be unfavourable for a visit to the island, turned the boat's head towards Carrig, which they reached late in the evening. The partners in this criminal plot, which by the better feeling of the servant was frustrated on *this* occasion, now separated for a season, and John S—— and Elly moved about from place to place, the hardened villain, no doubt (according as his funds became exhausted), every day getting more determined, if he could not succeed in prevailing upon his servant to help him in perpetrating this deed of darkness, by some means to rid himself of his burden, and if necessary, to immolate her with his own hand. Several days passed away after this first failure of *Lieutenant* S—— in accomplishing his fell intent to sacrifice the gentle victim, whose support was now a burden too heavy for such a worthless wretch to bear, and the many privations which poor Elly had to undergo during her peregrinations from house to house told fearfully upon her delicate frame. Had the accomplished villain waited a little longer, the young creature would inevitably have sunk under her trials, and thus have saved the guilty wretch from adding the crime of murder to his other evil deeds. In the mean time Stephen S—— had taken the boat up to G——, where, as the noble river, which was the scene of this sad tragedy, washed its shores, several of the inhabitants, who possessed small craft like that belonging to this wretched man, earned a livelihood by fishing. Just after he had separated from his master, who was his partner in the boat, he spent some days fishing, and in one of his trips to Clonderalan Bay at the opposite side of the river (where flat-fish abounded), by a sudden lurch of the boat the large stone with the iron chain attached (which had been prepared for sinking the body of the poor girl, whom they had conspired to murder) fell overboard, and "sunk as lead in the mighty waters." To this apparently casual misadventure may probably be attributed the discovery of the foul crime, which shortly after was perpetrated. Had the chain, instead of the rope which was used in sinking the murdered remains of poor Elly, been attached to the body, it doubtless would have remained at the bottom of the river, till every limb should be severed; and though strong suspicion would probably have rested upon the perpetrators, her simple disappearance would never have sufficiently satisfied a jury so as to enable them to convict. How different was the case when the rotting of the rope enabled the body to rise to the surface, what fresh evidence of the crime did the finding of the remains, as before described, bring to light, supported by the sworn testimony of J—— K—— at the coroner's inquest, that the very rope had been his property, which he lent to John S—— and Stephen S——; that he knew it by his own splicing; above all, the evidence of Ellen W——, as to the double sockets for the teeth; the discovery of the victim's clothing with the relatives of Stephen S——, together with sundry other facts almost demonstrative of the guilt of the accused. With such a mass of clear circumstantial evidence no intelligent jury could refuse to convict, or entertain any reasonable doubt that the prisoners who were arraigned were guilty of the dreadful crime which was laid to their charge. After Stephen S—— had returned from his fishing excursion he made up his mind again to seek out his master, who, bad as he felt he was himself, he thought was much worse, and would doubtless endeavour somehow to be revenged upon him, if he did not strive to play him off, and give him hope that he would yet be his instrument in completing this hellish plot. Though Stephen S—— was by far the more powerful man of the two, and in fair stand-up fight would easily have worsted John S——, still, knowing what a desperate villain the latter was, he feared that he might some time take him unawares, knock him on the head, and thus get rid of one who knew almost all his secret thoughts. Had this unfortunate wretch had the manliness and moral courage to shake off this diabolical companion, whose superior rank, instead of being used for good, exercised an evil dominion over his unhappy associate in crime, he might have been rescued from the criminal practices which he was following, and from the ignominious death which he so justly suffered. But no! he seemed spell-bound by this unrelenting and cruel man, and in an evil hour was made the instrument of perpetrating this dark deed of blood, which at the time it was committed, now nearly fifty years ago, struck the whole community with the most unutterable horror. Never that I am aware (except in the novel* and drama,† which have given very imperfect sketches of the facts) has this dark tragedy been chronicled in the garb of a true and faithful history of

* *Gerald Griffin's Collegians.*
† *The Colleen Bawn.*

the sad occurrence, as a personal knowledge of almost every fact here recorded has now enabled me to do. The author of this narrative, though now in the sere and yellow leaf, and fast verging towards that bourne from whence there is no return, is still, blessed be God, robust beyond the vast majority of his equals in years, and his memory of the facts he has related, as clear and retentive as it was on that eventful day when he saw poor Elly's mutilated remains consigned to the grave. Let not the reader of this sad history say the author is canting when, in this brief episode, he earnestly tries to warn his youthful friends against giving way to the promptings of their naturally evil hearts, or yielding to the manifold temptations to which they are constantly exposed. Let the fate of Lieutenant John S———, the once admired companion of the nobility and gentry of the county Limerick, afford an awful warning to those proud boasters whose end is frequently destruction, and who too often glory in their shame.

G

How little did this convicted felon, when joining at the festive board in the unseemly jest or ribald song (which at the time I now refer to were prominent features at their convivial gatherings), think that while the cheerful, and too often inebriating, glass went round, he was rushing upon his fate. While he thus stimulated his ungodly passions, he was sowing the deadly seed which at a future time would spring up in all its fetid rankness, would stupify every sense of moral right and wrong, and lead him to the commission of the fearful crime which he perpetrated without compunction, and justly expiated on the gallows.

CHAPTER IX.

When Stephen S—— had again resolved to rejoin his diabolical master, an hour's run, with a strong tide in his favour, brought him from his fishing ground to the western island, which was the principal resort of this dark conspirator. Poor, harassed Elly still lived, but was now reduced to a mere skeleton, the shadow of what she was when seduced from the home of her uncle, to whom she was deeply attached, and whose aged heart was well nigh broken since she fled from his roof. Immediately after his arrival John S—— renewed his proposal to carry out the dreadful design to get rid of the poor girl, and to possess themselves of the little property, composed of clothing and jewels, which she still retained. Bad as the wretched man, whom he used every means to employ as his agent to complete his nefarious plot, was, he remonstrated with him against the crime of murder, and proposed to return her to her sorrowing relatives, and to take all the blame upon himself. In case she should object against that, he said he would endeavour to prevail upon her to emigrate with himself to America, whither, as the reader may recollect, she told the author of this narrative, during his first interview with her, she was anxious and willing to go. To these proposals John S—— resolutely objected, and lest at any time an attempt should be made (after the fashion of Yelverton against Yelverton, of late notoriety) to establish the legitimacy of his marriage, nothing short of her immolation would satisfy this ruthless villain. To work therefore again he went, and after plying Stephen S—— with a large quantity of inebriating liquor, he persuaded poor unsuspecting Elly, whose health was greatly undermined, under the pretext of her taking a short row for the sake of the fresh air, to embark in the boat with Stephen S——; while he feigned illness himself, and promised that, after she spent an hour or so on the water, if he felt himself better, he would join her for another excursion. Just before they pushed off from the shore he took an opportunity of speaking in a whisper to Stephen S——, who was then well plied with strong drink, and while charging him not to return without doing the job, he turned on him a withering and determined look, and in handing him a bottle of whiskey he vehemently swore that if he came back to him with Elly alive he would surely be avenged. When this threat was delivered he handed him a gun* which he was to use as an instrument of death, immediately after which Stephen S—— pushed off the boat, his poor doomed victim being his only companion. While he pulled stoutly away towards mid-channel, which would be

---

* The very gun alluded to above I had in my hand the day I sailed down the river Shannon in company with Lieutenant S—— and poor Elly, shortly after the elopement.

at least four miles from the land, as his light bark skimmed swiftly over the water, he occasionally took a gulp of the intoxicating liquor from the bottle to nerve him to the performance of the dread deed, which in his sober senses he revolted against and could not bring himself to perform. Poor Elly, whose rest had of late been frequently disturbed, and her body enervated from a withdrawal of the comforts which she had been accustomed to in her uncle's house, had fallen fast asleep, her arm was resting on the gunwale of the boat, when the desperate villain, taking advantage of her unconsciousness, struck her a fearful blow with the but-end of the gun, which, though intended for her head, only reached her arm, which immediately hung broken and helpless by her side. The poor affrighted creature, thus suddenly and painfully roused to fearful consciousness, for the first time, no doubt, saw her real danger, and all at once felt the whole force of the conspiracy which was formed against her life. With a heartrending shriek, which the ruthless murderer confessed was ever after ringing in his ears, she cried out for mercy; but alas! her cries and entreaties were in vain. The desperate villain, excited almost to madness by the quantity of whiskey he had drank, with the fear of his atrocious master before his eyes, the almost certain fate which awaited him at his hands if he brought her back alive, and, in case by any means he should escape his vengeance, the certain penalty he would inevitably pay to the outraged laws of his country, determined to finish what in his drunken fury he had begun. He repeated his blows with unfailing hand till he had completed the work of death, and left the poor, unhappy girl a frightful shattered corpse at the bottom of the boat. The murder, long discussed between the guilty parties, having now been completed, what was the next step to be taken by the cruel perpetrator? Every article of clothing of any value was immediately stripped from her poor, crushed, mutilated body, and only a tightly laced bodice* and the under garment, which it would take too much time and trouble to remove, remained. It was then Stephen S—— felt the loss of the heavy stone and chain which, as before related, fell overboard on one of his fishing excursions. What was now to supply their place? As an overruling Providence would have it, the very rope which was sworn to by Jack K—— at the inquest, was extemporized. One of the largest stones amongst those which were used for ballast in the boat was laid hold of, the rope was tied as firmly to it as time would permit, and as soon as the wretched murderer had bound the neck and leg together (in which condition I saw the body after it was thrown ashore) he attached his poor victim to the rope and flung her overboard. The intoxicated villain now made for Carrig Island, where the prime mover, and more than equally guilty conspirator,

* The above articles of clothing I saw on the body when it was exhumed at the coroner's inquest.

was waiting, and having reached the shore he fully related to him all the particulars of the bloody work which he had done. Though John S—— did not see the death blows of the assassin, or hear the groans of the dying victim, he felt assured that she was no more, as he had narrowly watched the progress of the boat from the time it left the beach till it reached the spot where the murder was committed. Having clearly seen that no other craft came near it from the time it left, and having never taken his eyes from it till it returned to shore, without poor Elly, who had left the land alive, he made certain that the deed he had so long plotted had been done, and therefore heaped praises on the felon who had so faithfully carried out his behests. To reward him for his obedience to his orders, he now bestowed on him a portion of the ill-gotten spoils, in addition to which, when they returned to G——, Lieutenant S—— gave Mary S——, the sister of the actual murderer (as sworn to in her depositions now before me), a shift, a pair of shoes, a pocket, a cap, and a ribbon. The deponent also stated that she saw a plain gold ring on Stephen S——'s finger, and a figured one with Lieutenant S——, with whom also she saw four gold guineas, and a red leather pocket-book, all of which, on the trials, were sworn to by Ellen W—— as having belonged to poor Elly. When she inquired about his wife, as Elly was called, Lieutenant S—— first told her that he had left her with his sister at Kilkee, a bathing-place on the western coast, and afterwards, when she learned that this was untrue, he said that she had gone off with the captain of a ship. All that I have here related came to light after the conviction and condemnation of Stephen S——, who was to be executed in a few days, and contains the substance of his confession, and his full corroboration of the general features of the two trials, and the depositions of the witnesses on each occasion. From this nothing could induce him to swerve, and lest, as he said himself, his last hours upon earth should be disturbed by any entreaties (no matter from what quarter coming) to alter the statement he had made, or to lead any one to imagine, by word or hint from him, that Lieutenant S—— was innocent of the crime for which he suffered, reiterated his assertion that he had instigated him to commit the murder; and I believe it is a maxim of law that the conspirator is equally guilty with the perpetrator. He also sent a petition to the judges who tried him, acknowledging the full justice of his sentence, and requesting, at the same time, that he should not be interrupted by the visits of any persons except those whom he might, with the permission of the authorities, wish himself to converse with. This dying request of the unhappy man was strictly complied with, and when the fatal day arrived he publicly declared his guilt upon the scaffold, and stated, in the presence of thousands, that he had committed the fearful crime at the instigation of Lieutenant John S——; with whom, in an evil hour, he had cast in his lot, and in whose drunken orgies and vile practices, he had too readily joined. After this confession, the wretched murderer was launched into eternity, and paid the penalty of the dreadful crime he had committed by a violent and ignominious death at the common place of execution. The clear confession, and closing scene of Stephen S——'s wretched life, will show the reader the fearful nature of the determined denial of his guilt which sent Lieutenant John S—— into eternity with an awful lie upon his lips. "I thought," he said (as before mentioned), when the cap was removed for a few minutes from his eyes, "I should never see the light of heaven again. May the gates of Paradise be for ever shut against me if I had hand, act or part, in the crime for which I am about to die!" Oh, terrible addition to the many crimes with which his unhappy soul was stained! How hardened to every sense of that contrition for guilt which is often professed by some of the most uneducated criminals. It is almost incredible to think that one brought up in the light of a gentleman, who had served the Crown for many years in a military capacity, who, from his rank and station in life, must have known the procedure of our criminal courts, could have so deceived himself as to imagine that his obstinacy would have saved him. He may have served as a juror himself, he certainly had been an auditor of some of the trials of that disorganized period, when many Whiteboys and Rockites paid the penalty of their transgressions on the scaffold. He knew full well that several whose guilt was as clear as the noon-day sun, denied it to the last, and yet could not escape the sentence of the law. How such a man could vainly imagine that a hardened denial, like his, would save his life is almost utterly unaccountable. Thus the curtain fell over one of the most distressing tragedies that ever was enacted in Ireland, the remembrance of which is so fresh in my mind's eye after nearly half a century that I can even now trace the lineaments of nearly every face in the drama. I almost feel that it was but yesterday that I issued from the gates of old Trinity; that I sat beside Jim Dempsey on the coach-box; that I helped to put out the fire in the house in Limerick; that I sailed down the river Shannon with Lieutenant S—— and poor Elly; that I saw her again at Kilrush, and had a hearty greeting from her; that I shortly after saw her mutilated remains, and was cognizant of all the facts connected with the trial and execution of her murderers. Having now faithfully related the most prominent features, and in my opinion most touching scenes in this remarkable tragedy, I shall close my sketch by once more appealing to the good feelings, especially, of my youthful readers, who perhaps, often in their hot pursuit of pleasure, too easily yield to the romantic ideas which the sensation novels of the present day are apt to inoculate them with. The consequences, though it may be they are lightly thought of, have a tendency, in a variety of ways,